Life itself is simple, but without exception,
we all tend to complicate it.
If you want to participate in this learning experience,
you can share the book's contents with whomever you wish.

Cover illustration created specially for this book
by the Spanish painter Conrado.

Order this book online at www.trafford.com
or email orders@trafford.com

Most Trafford titles are also available at major online book retailers.

Note for Librarians: A cataloguing record for this book is available from Library
and Archives Canada at www.collectionscanada.ca/amicus/index-e.html

Printed in Victoria, BC, Canada.

ISBN: 978-1-4251-8712-5 (Soft)
ISBN: 978-1-4269-1997-8 (e-book)

*Our mission is to efficiently provide the world's finest, most comprehensive
book publishing service, enabling every author to experience success.
To find out how to publish your book, your way, and have it available
worldwide, visit us online at www.trafford.com*

Trafford rev. 9/25/2009

 www.trafford.com

North America & international
toll-free: 1 888 232 4444 (USA & Canada)
phone: 250 383 6864 ♦ fax: 812 355 4082

LIFE IS SIMPLE

This book is dedicated to those who are
anxious to understand life and thereby
discover and acknowledge their own
creativity.

LIFE IS SIMPLE

Xamanda La Chou

Life; books; visits to Asia, South America, Europe, and to the Native Americans of the United States; the exchange of knowledge and experience with other 'seekers;' the many seminars I have participated in; and most of all, listening to my inner voice: all of this has led me to express in this book the many insights I have gleaned in life from **my own point of view**. But where does this inner voice get the information from? Maybe it has a direct connection to the *Akashic records*, which is another way of 'communicating with God.'

This is **my** book. If you read it and integrate it into your life it will probably challenge your own principles of life and your belief system and so little by little you will 'write' **your own** book. Have fun with it! We will have something in common and each of us will enjoy it in our own way.

Xamanda La Chou

INTRODUCTION

(I start this book with "It was on a Friday" instead of "Once upon a Friday" because only children believe in fairy tales. But since this is perhaps a story for grown-ups, I would like it to reach everyone's inner child)...

It was on a Friday evening around eight o'clock, in the beginning of September, when I got a phone call from a lady whom I met in the Philippines while observing some faith-healers operate on patients with their bare hands to cure them.

Hi, how are you? I'm Xamanda La Chou; we met in the Philippines.

Oh, Yes! You're the one with the lost gaze and long blonde hair. I remember you very well.

Do you remember when we chatted about reality, illusion and many other topics about life? You gave me your card, so I'm calling to ask a favor of you. All through the conversations we had, I realized you are a man who is open to the spiritual and esoteric worlds. I've written a manuscript about life **from my own point of view**. Since this world manifests itself based on duality, I'm looking for a man who has lived his life through the eyes of my manuscript and who would like to publish it.

I find this proposal quite interesting and I'd love to have this experience. I have often thought about you too, because I was very impressed by your ideas. I think I've come a long way since then.

I would like you to read my manuscript, apply it to your everyday life and share it with your friends. Afterwards, I'd like us to get together again sometime. And then I'd like you to ask me questions as my interviewer and I will answer you based on my manuscript.

Ah, great! I'd love it! Then I will wait for you to send it to me so I can read it and contribute my share. I'll wait for you to get in touch with me again, since I have neither your address nor your phone number.

Sure, no problem. When the time is right, I'll get in touch with you and we'll see each other somewhere in Europe.

OK, fantastic!

Great! Thanks a lot and have fun with life – until then!

The Interviewer

LIFE IS SIMPLE

Hi Xamanda! What a beautiful place this is, where we can see the plains illuminated by all this lightening! Tonight a strong and beautiful storm is brewing, transforming night to day. I believe this is a good omen for starting this book. Let's see what happens.

I'll write down my notes. Later I will analyze and maybe expand them from my conversations with friends. Agreed? Very well, let's get started:

What is your main philosophy on life?

Well, *"Life is Simple"* is the title of this book – because if we go to its roots, life actually is very simple.

Yes, I agree, but do please elaborate:

Why is life simple?

Of course, it depends on the point of view from which you approach life. It matters what *you believe*, because you have either a half-full, or half-empty glass. Since I like the half-full glass, my philosophy on life is simple. Usually, people cannot quite say that life is simple, but from *my* point of view it sure is because...

I carry full responsibility for my own life.

The essential questions about who I am and what life has in store for me, have moved me to write this book about life.

In this process I have realized the following:

I have no influence over anyone.

I have no responsibility for anyone.

I alone am my life's creator.
I alone have written the book of my life.

These are the basis of my life. From here, we will soon see how we realize that *life is indeed simple.*

Xamanda, I recall you mentioning other possible titles for this book, such as:

'Help yourself, because no one else can – not even God'.

This title is very interesting. Another possibility you gave was:

'My glass is half full – and yours?'

The 'half-full/half-empty' philosophy has always fascinated me! Knowing that both the glass and the contents are always one and the same, it depends only on your viewpoint which of the two you choose.

This is why I have asked you to look for an artist capable of capturing, through his art, the mystical message that the *glass* philosophy carries, so that we all can sense a part of our own essence.

Good! Another one that fascinated me was:

'The mosaic says it all'.

The idea of the mosaic is very profound. Viewing it from a few steps back, one can see how life is simple.

Among the variety of titles, the one that impacted me most – and even gave me goose bumps was:

'To comprehend the human being, we must first comprehend God'.

Now I have a question for you – since you speak of comprehending God:

Who is God for you?

God is everything. You are God, I am God – we all are God. The point is that according to the Bible and many other belief systems of the world, God is almighty, all knowing and eternal – without beginning or end. And this word *'all'* – **which includes 'nothing'** – is the basis of the most fundamental idea. Therefore, God is *all*. But can we put ourselves in God's shoes? For a human being it is almost impossible, even though we will try.

God is almighty and all-knowing. He is everything – **and at the same time - nothing**. God doesn't exclude *nothingness*. We could, then, even say that *everything is nothing*. From a human point of view, this is very hard to understand. But if we put ourselves in God's place, for Him everything is instantaneous – that is, time does **not yet** exist. *So,* **for God to know Himself, he must NOT know Himself. And He knows that He doesn't know Himself**. This sounds odd, but we should delve a little deeper into this concept.

Even God has asked the most famous question: **Who am I?** *I'm God.* But nothing moves in His universe, for God knows He is everything, so He can be anyone He wants to be. He can be Peter Pan, Einstein, an E.T – it doesn't matter since He is everything. If He asks himself, **what am I?** Still nothing moves there in God's world. Because He can be a tomato, a banana, a lake, a UFO – anything He wants to be.

What moved and created this world?

The Bible helps us out a bit: *In the beginning was the Word,* ('the Word' is also interpreted as *logos*, meaning 'thought-action,' or *intention*). *And the Word was with God, and* **the Word was God**. So...

What could this word be?

The Bible also indicates that **we should be as children**. What is the difference between children and adults? Perhaps it is *innocence*, keeping the form of the inner child who is always asking, *why?* Aha!

WHY?

I believe the question God asked Himself is *Why: Why am I a banana and not a human being?* Or: *why am I a tree and not a star? Why am I ugly and not handsome? Why am I a man and not a woman? Why? Why? Why?* And we all know the dilemma of *why*: we are being asked *why* and we really don't know the answer. So, here's how something finally moved in God's world: in order to satisfy His **curiosity**, He created our Universe.

Xamanda, you say that we truly don't know the answer to the question 'why?' – for example, the question 'why am I a man and not a woman?' Can you explain this a bit more?

Of course! In the world of God (who knows everything), the unknown does not exist, *while it also exists*. So the question, *why am I a man and not a woman?* doesn't exist. Because in God's world, a man is a man because he is man. A woman is a woman because she is a woman. This can also be applied to this world of human beings! For Him, comparison doesn't exist. But in order to compare, to know this answer, **he had to create something outside of himself – a limited God**. *This 'something' is the human being.* Therefore, we have been created in this world of duality.

What is this duality you talk about so often?

Duality exists between *yes* and *no*, *good* and *bad*, *above* and *below*, *white* and *black*, *inside* and *outside*, *yin* and *yang*, **love and fear** (not hatred, for fear creates hatred) – all of this and so much more. Thus comparing, evaluating and judging, is where we humans come in, because **God is not capable of having an experience:** as He knows everything and is everything, He cannot experience what it means to be ugly and not pretty, intelligent and not foolish simultaneously – according to the viewpoint of who is judging. This is why He has created this dualistic world just for us human beings, whom He created in His image. We are God and at the same time we are not God. The **not-God part** is the human being's mind; **the God part** is the human being's heart.

The conscious mind, as seat of the *ego*, is divided between the right hemisphere – the feminine aspect, which is intuition and emotions; and the left hemisphere – the masculine aspect, which is intellect, reason, judgment and comparison. The human being in the heart is God manifesting himself in *simple being* – without judging. We simply *are*. "*Feeling*" is the mystical cord that connects both hemispheres, as normally the hemispheres cannot communicate with each other.

I've read in your manuscript that you distinguish between feeling and emotion.

According to the dictionary, *feeling* is something experienced at the soul-level that you take part in without judging, whereas *emotion* is the reaction to something. Emotions are created by the ego. The greater the ego, the more it gets caught up in mental activity, by reasoning (comparing and judging). *"The judge"* can't live without labeling everything. For example, we feel sad simply because we feel sad – and for no other reason. But the ego is not content with this, so because of this sadness (or perhaps even joy, or whatever), which comes from the heart, the ego will immediately ask itself, *why am I sad?* Or, *why am I happy? Why? Why? Why?* – And it offers us many reasons, many labels, transforming the feeling into **emotion**.

The ego cannot exist in *feeling* because its capacity is only binary, i.e., the brain sends the ego-being only *'yes'* and *'no'* – although at very high speed. Apparently, according to current science, the brain processes some three-to-five-hundred thousand million bits of information per second. But the conscious mind can only be aware of, or work with, two-to-five thousand bits per second. That is to say, the part unknown to us, the subconscious mind, is very much greater than the conscious mind. In other words, the conscious mind's capacity is as ten centimeters compared to the brain's capacity of over twenty thousand kilometers. The playground of the ego is situated only in the conscious mind.

According to current science, the expression of emotions is nothing more than chemical reactions that make holographic memories in our brain, interfacing with many programs that make us **react** emotionally. For many people, emotions and feelings are the same thing.

The creation of the ego is one of the laws God has given to enable us to be separate from Him – which actually we are not. But this life is an illusion that only exists because we believe we are separate from God, that we are not God, that we are simply human beings – something distinct from God. That is to say, we have to forget that we are God.

Xamanda, you also speak about the fundamental laws of this life that make it possible for this dualistic world of ours that we experience so intensely to exist. Tell me more...

What laws make this world real?

Of course! One of these laws is:

The duality of this world is composed of 50% positive and 50% negative.

This is hard to understand, but according to my experience, each time someone does something "good," simultaneously, someone else does something "bad," so that balance is preserved. The art of life is to find positivity behind negativity using the laws of duality. (There is no ill by which some good does not come).

Another law is:

We are what we believe we are.

In this way our belief is what makes our being in this world possible. Although sometimes, we do not believe what we believe: I don't believe in witches, but nevertheless they exist! (Contradiction). Think about such sayings as these: "Faith can move mountains" or: "Faith will heal you." – Likewise, if a belief is harmful, it will make you ill!

Another of these laws is:

The same is never the same.

No two things in this world are alike. Of course there are no two men or women alike; it is imperative that we realize we are all **unique individuals**, who will each have to know and live our own individualities. But obviously, in this duality there are forces that try to make us alike; this is part of the game called life.

Another law is:

There exists neither past nor future – nor the present itself, but only the moment.

We are not even capable of thinking in terms of the present time either, because the thought you just had is already in the past, and as the past doesn't exist, so then we can only recall memories of the past – and project a memory as what we will in the future.

There are many books about "living in the present." But we should realize that we are incapable of being in the present – since it is only a memorized holographic image of what we just thought. Therefore at the moment of thought we just recreate a **similar image – but it's never exactly the same.**

As we have already seen, **truth exists only in the fact that something is as it is,** and as we are all individuals, **we each have our own truth,** the truth that we believe to be the truth. From this perspective, **we all hold the truth** – we are all right – and here we enter the war of egos: *I am more right than you are*, or *I'm right and you're not*. This is also the basis for living in duality. However, in reality, we *all* are right because we are God and God is all-knowing. Therefore it is not possible for us to be mistaken. But the paradox is that in not erring, we do err.

Xamanda, if all of us were right, then we would have no problems; nevertheless, I see that almost everybody in this world has so many problems.

Of course! *Having* problems is *believing* that you have problems, but the truth is there are only solutions – right and wrong ones. You must think of the brain as a binary computer that is only capable of distinguishing between *yes* and *no* – of course at a very fast rate.

When we come up with an idea that we believe, our subconscious mind **re**acts to the belief. As we have many beliefs, each one of them is like a program and some-times some of them oppose each other. Here is where the human being comes under stress. Depending on which belief is the strongest, one program will be more effective than the other. Since programs cannot be erased, but only deactivated, 'reprogramming' can be achieved through feeling, living, and accepting these fundamental laws of the universe: that we are all individuals and that we each have the right to be as we are. But, as we have seen, it is very hard to know the answer to *Who am I?* We all bring into this world our natural intelligence (not necessarily intellectual intelligence). We all need to find out what our gift is. What would I like to do in this life? What are my weaknesses, which at the same time, could turn out to be my strengths? What have I come here to experience? When we don't know, the whole mechanism can be very hard to understand, because we can easily get lost in all those programs that we acquire throughout the process of life.

We have come to this world having chosen our parents. So, at conception we begin being programmed. Our basic program consists of being innocent, having fun, living freely and doing whatever we want without harming anyone. But at conception (as we will see later, in the astrology chapter), we are already receiving information – programs in our subconscious mind that make us a certain way that may not necessarily be of our own essence.

For many – especially for mothers, accepting the truth that we have chosen our parents is tremendously powerful.

I also had this experience. I remember very well, Xamanda, when I told my mother that she had chosen her parents – Ouch! It was one of the worst clashes of our relationship; she hated her father and couldn't accept the notion of having chosen him herself!

Yes, this happens quite often, but maybe if we accept and digest such information, we could certainly heal many wounds.

During pregnancy, we receive a lot of information from our parents and from the environment. For instance: we sense and feel how well they get along or whether we are a wanted child, etc. There is even a whole philosophy surrounding the subject of prenatal experiences.

After feeling safe, warm, and loved inside the womb for quite some time, we get the rude shock of entering this world. As soon as we are born we are even forced to cry. From then on, many influences never cease programming us and altering our true essence. Above all, the mother exerts great influence on our life and our dependence on her can last a lifetime, with all its consequences.

I'm quite intrigued by what you said regarding the mother's role.

Yes, I can well understand it. Instinctively the mother knows that the newborn baby is her own flesh and blood, part of her own body. Everything is hers, absolutely independently from the man's physical contribution, which might be a few tiny hairs, if anything at all!

Being a mother of three, I know what I'm talking about. Generally, the mother, ostensibly out of love, never gives up protection or possession of her children throughout her whole life. This is why her programming of our innocent being is so strong. The mother's influence superimposes itself on the child's character; the umbilical cord is only cut off physically, almost never psychologically and somehow we feel influenced by her – as if by remote control – even to the day we die! As we will also see in the astrological section, the moon represents the mother at the time of the delivery, while the sun represents the father. All of this leaves many impressions.

I prefer to say *conditioning* – for if we only talk about *programming* we may think we are just robots, which have only ones and zeros.

So far, we have only been speaking in terms of the influences on our conscious and subconscious minds, not the heart, which has neither judgment nor comparison, since it is the center of love.

Let's discuss what LOVE really is. Thousands of books have been written about love, and we're always talking about it. But hardly anyone ever says what it really is. Everyone has a different image of what *love* means, but I think the simplest expression of true love would be:

I accept whom I love as they are, rather than as I want them to be.

Immediately one can see that this is an altogether different mode of operation from its common substitutes. It can't be just a program, since our natural essence is to accept things just as they are – accepting ourselves as we are.

After the mother, we receive conditioning by the father's influence. Often the children compete with him or the father competes with the children, because now at home, his lover has transformed into a mother and he feels he'll lose part of what he has had with her till now. It is very natural, but few women understand this process in which mothers devote themselves so strongly to their new "property." Therefore the role of being wife and mother is very crucial.

The instinct of motherhood has no intention of consciously or unconsciously letting go of her children – much less, cutting the psychological 'umbilical cord.' The cord between mother and son is especially strong.

For example, it is clearly observed in the horoscope, that men, when they go looking for a partner, are actually looking for some aspect of the mother – in much the same way that women look for the 'image' of their father in a mate. This of course, creates new conflicts.

Later there is additional conditioning from family, society and teachers, which are also quite influential. All of these influences call for learning more than understanding, basically favoring the left hemisphere with its intellect. Normally, no one teaches us **how** to learn. An important learning method is looking up the root meaning of a word that we don't understand. For example, not knowing the meaning of the word *mathematics* can block one's interest in – and understanding of – the subject. Even though we come into this world with a natural intelligence, through the course of life we lose touch with it and we are imprisoned by whatever system we happen to end up in.

Obviously later experiences with friends and coworkers condition us, as well as those with partners. This is how we become a melting pot of so many influences that we sometimes get really lost – reacting more than acting – and nearly losing all of our natural essence.

But we can never lose an experience; it remains in each cell of our body. Our life, identity, and experiences are all there. To remember who we are, we can use meditation. To be one with nature, to hug and feel a tree can be very healing as well. This book is meant to somehow point the way to reestablish and rediscover that pure essence that we are.

Xamanda, are there any techniques to help us return to our essence, to reunite with who we really are and the reason we came here to Earth?

Yes, one is astrology; meditation and the realization that we are God are two more. In the esoteric scene there are so many ways of healing oneself. One that most impresses me is...

The image of the mosaic.

For me, this is one of the most phenomenal secrets. The mosaic is composed of many pebbles, some white, some black and also many other colors. Some of these pebbles form a cloud, some a house, the sun, maybe some people. But since we are human beings, we will meet many people through out life.

So, all these pebbles represent *us*. It is exactly the same as with the mosaic: when we step back a bit, a completely new image appears before our eyes, which is much more than the sum total of the pebbles. And the marvelous existence of this image that the message the mosaic shows us, really fascinates me.

When I do an astral chart reading, for a while I feel – with great pleasure – almost the whole basic essence of a being through all the information I get – just like the mosaic.

Another way of knowing oneself better is:

The mirror method.

Oh yes, the mirror! Ouch again! This too has taken me a long time to understand, but I see that this method is one of the richest in terms of information.

Yes, the mirror's image is the outside's resonance with our inside. But nothing outside can resonate with us emotionally if we have no counterpart **within**. The outside world is the mirror of our internal world. The way we perceive it is the way we see ourselves, whether from the positive or the negative side of life. This is very hard to accept because sometimes the mirror reflects very ugly aspects of our self. The images and themes of violence, morbidity, terror, etc., that we see are very hard to associate with our inner self, thus, many people don't want to believe that this mirror method is true. However, it is a very simple truth, because we are so unique. We are the creator of our own world and we have no power whatsoever to influence others, as I mentioned before.

As a matter of fact, according to new findings, we never *actually touch* each other at all, which is also astonishing. If I touch your arm, our bodies are actually far from physically touching; only the *intention* of touching reaches the conscious mind by creating a chemical reaction of 'touch' in our brains. Note that this has nothing to do with the aura, which is an energy field *surrounding* the physical body. Matter, that is, the atom, is so small that it is only an infinitesimal point in this universe. For those who want to learn more about this, there are plenty of books and even movies about this subject.

Everything is just an experience and for me the word *experience* is the essence of our lives. If we quit judging, then everything is just an experience, so the worst thing that can ever happen is just an experience. Without *our* experiences, God cannot experience.

Through the mirror, we see the outside world. A vast amount of information floods us, every bit of which resonates with many of our internal programs. Likewise, **the law of resonance**, **the law of chaos**, and **the law of order in chaos** are fascinating ways to understand this life.

Another technique to restore our essence is:

Quieting the mind.

There are a lot of people who are bothered by something that happened to them that they were unable to immediately take responsibility for.

A very helpful method is to mock the ego's intelligence (so to speak) by practicing **"false calculation."** For instance, 5 plus 3 is 523, minus 3 is 1300, plus 5 is -5, plus 33 is 1320, etc. When you do this deliberately, you will practically short-circuit your ego's logical mind, because it gets hopelessly lost, allowing you to recuperate and take a break for a little while. Also, giving the ego an order to read a blank page produces a similar effect. The truth is, everything is an illusion of the ego, which exists solely for this experience that we call life.

Man is always competing. A lot of people need to compete; it is simply an ego-game that only feeds our vices. Not knowing how to stop anxiety forms vices. But we are not in control. Therefore, for me to compete is to lose, because both lose.

There is a meeting point in all human relationships, where egos can be in agreement and where both win and both are right. But as we've already seen in the mirror example, if someone tells you: "you're an idiot" – he's really telling this to himself. We mistakenly take it personally. Right? Because maybe we have also said it to others and thus the law of resonance is set into motion. A very fundamental truth is that we all speak to ourselves. Look at all the people talking like parrots – like me for instance; I'm telling all of this to myself.

And this is a very special moment where I would like to point out that I'm writing this book for myself alone. If anyone wants to participate in it and maybe learn from it, it's their choice and responsibility. That is why there is no copyright on anything I'm saying here; I simply invite you to share it.

One subject we still haven't touched on yet is **illness,** which ultimately has its roots in psychological imbalance. This subject is very broad and there are plenty of books that deal with it.

I believe that we are capable of curing and healing ourselves. Illness is the body crying out, warning us that we have not listened to our inner voice and that we are wandering from our source, our own essence. Illness also stems from using **poor me** power to be at the center of attention and get sympathy. Under those conditions we feel very weak and unable to receive affection from others. So we get taken care of by getting sick.

I want to tell you a story I learned from a friend, so I know it's true:

My friend's friend was diagnosed with cancer and given only four-to-five weeks to live. He was a very special person who talked very kindly, never lost his temper, and was truly appreciated for who he was. One night after he was told of his illness, he was out driving when he stopped at a traffic light. A woman got into his car and wanted to rob him. He placed his hands on his head and started saying "this is unbelievable, I am dying and now I am being robbed!". His face turned red as a beet, as if his head was going to explode. It was only then that he started to defend himself. He blasted her with a lifetime of stored-up anger and knocked her out of the car door with his fists!

A few days later, the doctors ran more tests on him and found him to be completely healthy. For the first time in his life this man let himself express his negative emotions to survive!

So here we see that the way an illness manifests can show us where and how we have been unfaithful to ourselves.

Xamanda, I think now is a good opportunity to finish this part; we have reached a point where more could become less. We have enough information for the moment, for us to absorb, experience, practice and share!

Agreed! Just as in any good mystery novel, everything is elegantly resolved in the last few pages, I also want to offer you the magical key and a quick way to keep life simple: Just as the word *why* got us into this "chaotic" life and by the law of duality, there must be another escape word, which is...

SO WHAT!

Hah! Hah! Hah! And how it works! How freeing!

Since life will seduce us time and again to jump back into the hustle and bustle of human existence, this time we will do it in a more conscious way and even learn to have fun with it.

APPENDICES

1. COCKTAILS

INGREDIENTS: Your phone call, a parking space, the rain, roses, my neighbor, chocolate, the sun, ten extra pounds, watching TV or reading the newspapers, influences from others, the necessity of communication, work, individuality, self esteem, teenagers, cities, people and their education.

Since life is a mixture of experiences which essentially depend on everybody's viewpoint, here are two different cocktails: one tasted from the half-empty glass, the other one from the half-full glass – both enhanced by various emotions.

THE "BAD VIBE" COCKTAIL

- Darn! She's calling me again.

- I can never find a parking space.

- It rains all the time, especially when I don't have my umbrella.

- Roses always have thorns and they wilt so fast.

- My neighbor is a pain in the neck and his sons are always so noisy.

- Chocolate makes me fat.

- The sun ages my skin.

- Your ten extra pounds make you look fat and ugly.

- I need the adrenaline I get from watching TV and reading the newspapers, because it makes me realize that a lot of people are worse off than I am.

- My life is influenced by others; which usually makes me feel like a 'poor me' person.

- Chatting with other people can be very annoying, especially when I'm not the center of attention.

- I only work because I need the money.

- You are selfish because you refuse to do what I ask you to do.

- Nobody likes me and everybody just wants to take advantage of me.

- Teenagers always want to go out and have a good time instead of focusing on their future.

- Cities are overpopulated and filled with bad energy.

- People without a college education are dumb and boring.

Mix all these ingredients with the conviction that life is a heavy burden even though there are occasional happy moments.

THE "GOOD VIBE" COCKTAIL

- I'm always glad when you call.

- There's always a parking space waiting for mc.

- Rain can be romantic, and above all, is good for nature.

- Roses are beautiful and most have a pleasant fragrance; it's a wonderful flower.

- I seldom talk to my neighbor, but his wife is very nice and their children are very lively.

- I love chocolate; it doesn't make me fat because I just don't believe it does.

- The sun gives me energy.

- Your extra ten pounds invite me to caress you.

- Instead of watching TV or reading the newspaper, I feel better after reading a book or taking a walk in nature.

- When I organize my life with pleasure and joy, it is easier to assume responsibilities.

- I am always interested in what others have to say – I already know what I have to say!

- I like to work because it gives me great pleasure to be creative.

- I'm fascinated by the way you live your individuality; it seems to me that you are very true to yourself.

- I have good self-esteem, so I don't depend on others; they can give me what they want to and I can give them what I want.

- Teenagers are full of joy and are happy to experience life to the fullest.

- Fortunately most people live in cities; this way the countryside is more peaceful and nature is more enjoyable.

- One can learn a lot about life and nature through the wisdom of simple people.

Mix all these ingredients with the conviction that life is beautiful even though sometimes it doesn't seem so.

Realizing that in both cocktails, **the ingredients are the same,** we become aware that everything basically depends on the decisions we make.

2. MORE INFORMATION

Following are some interesting points of view to consider on our way towards a simple life:

- **We must evolve; we must educate ourselves and acquire much wisdom.** Obviously these are programs that divert us from our natural intelligence and place us more towards the left hemisphere of our brain and we lose connection with our intuition. To the contrary, the information we need usually comes by intuition – whenever we need it.

- In the esoteric world there's another subject: **Enlightenment.** During my trips and in the seminars I've attended, I have come across many people who are very interested in this. Nowadays, you can even talk to the enlightened through the web. Reading up on the subject can be very instructive and it may be very healing to devote yourself to it. But, as we all know, we already are enlightened, so aren't we seeking something we already have? It's like the dog chasing his own tail, isn't it? I think it is a very interesting game.

According to my own opinion, a person's stage of illumination depends on how he behaves in the relative handling of the dual energy forces - either positive or negative, thus showing the capacity to experience both forces as one.

- Another way to meet someone's truth is **walking in someone else's shoes.** There's a Native American saying that goes like this: *"Do not judge your neighbor until you walk two moons in his moccasins."*

Since we are perfect, there's no way we can be mistaken. We are capable of seeing another person's truth through his eyes. By doing this we comprehend the other because in **his** place we would do the same. The better we comprehend others, the better we comprehend ourselves. By looking through the eyes of another, we can – without judging – feel and perceive his inner life. This is quite revealing and through this, we can avoid creating opportunities for more fights. Furthermore, we know that criticism springs from insecurity, inferiority complex, including low self esteem acquired as a result of so much conditioning or whatever it is that motivates us to criticize others.

• As we will see, **the use of words can be very deceptive**. Seldom is anger soothed by many words. Sometimes a hug, or a simple handshake or an understanding glance will relieve it more easily.

There is a saying that goes **suffering shared is suffering halved** or **joy shared is double joy.** We all know this. That's why I always like to share with others everything in life that is beautiful and try to avoid sharing the negative aspects of this world.

For me, one of the most fulfilling and fun experiences is to bring out in others their inner child. Here we enter into the mentality of a child whose spirit is blooming with happiness, adventure, and innocence. He spontaneously recognizes: By golly! This looks fun! Wow!

- There is something else that limits us: **feeling guilty.** This stems from conditioning or from competing with the father. For example: "I cannot do all the things he expects me to do; I can't live up to his expectations." The same thing happens with partners. "I love her a lot but I think I'm not good enough for her" – not realizing that we must each satisfy ourselves first in order to be happy. *The mirror method teaches us that it is not possible to give that which we don't have.*

This internal guilt, or **the poor me,** makes us feel the need to be punished. I see this in a lot of people who are very unhappy, who feel guilty and worthless – **the poor me** – attracting negativity like a magnet. As I said, this world is ruled by 50% of the positive aspect or positive beings and 50% of the negative aspect or negative beings. Both the black energy and the white energy, are each fed by our information, our essence, our energy. Therefore if we "plug in" to the positive, we "feed" this positive aspect, but if, on the contrary, we "plug in" to the negative – for instance watching war or horror movies, violent news, and criticism – we get connected to the other pole and feed the negative aspect of this world. It is undoubtedly a game between these two forces.

• My inner voice has told me that there are **black masters** and **white masters**. The latter has to lower his high vibration because at that level we can not understand him and he has to turn "grey" to communicate with us. Black masters also have to turn "grey" to be able to communicate with us. It's not at all easy to find out the origin of the "grey." This is something that has always fascinated me; it has often made me smile when I hear or read books about channeling information through a medium. I realize that they too have to submit themselves to the duality laws of this world.

- Another subject is **freedom** which we will take a look at in the chapter on Astrology. Pisces is freedom in water and Aquarius is freedom in air. The drama that arises from seeking this freedom is the seeking itself. Either we are free or we are not free. We are always free; it is only our conditioning or our acceptance of many conditioning programs that make us forego or be unaware of that freedom. Freedom also means **liberating the ego, not liberation from the ego**!

I am free and I acknowledge myself for I have worked hard with these energies. Regarding the subject on energies, it is of utmost importance to know that science has confirmed that in this

Universe energy is never lost. The sum total of energy always remains the same; it just changes form. In other words, a fight has negative energy but the sum total of energy is the same; it is just that it has more negative than positive ones. And when a conflict is worked out and, for instance, two beings make peace, this negative energy converts to positive.

Our body is more-or-less 80% water. According to recent discoveries, **water is a messenger** – a medium of information – that can convert positive information into negative information, and vice-versa, depending on the conscious or unconscious intention of a human being – according to the half-empty or half-full point of view.

Due to conditioning, we acquire 'foreign energies' (from the mother or father, etc.). An example of this would be: "get out of the draft or it will make you sick." And when we are bothered, at any time we can mentally return our energies to their original state, cleansing and healing ourselves, taking responsibility for having accepted those thought-forms which we no longer want. This is the fundamental game of this life and of this Universe, which I think has no limits.

- One truth that really impresses me is: **Only the weak want to be strong** – it is never the other way around.

- As we have seen, all of life is nothing more than the sum total points of view. One of them is that **action creates abundance.** Not reaction. When we believe that there is abundance in the Universe and that we must focus all of our intention and faith on it, then we are bound to have abundance.

On the road to this abundance, however, there are very well-known and widely used words which impede us. They are obstacles, such as: *always, I wish, never, nobody, everybody, I would like, just in case,* etc. These words place stones in our way to abundance because the unconscious mind, which creates action, gets stuck in the "I wish" mode. So we provide ourselves with many "I wish" situations. Try to get away from negative affirmations and the desires themselves.

It is very important to be aware that these words can induce scarcity instead of abundance, and that selecting positive words is very helpful.

- A corollary of the mirror theory is also: **Who is our enemy?**

*I have a story regarding this subject: One day I was riding a car with my best friend and we were talking about his enemies and he said: "the more I think that my enemies can harm me, the more I realize that something is wrong with the notion that there's an enemy out there." Then I told him: "Yes, maybe you are realizing that **there is only one enemy in life**." He looked at me and burst out laughing – this was very memorable because the whole car was dancing side-to-side from so much laughter. "Yes, we are the only enemy we have in this world!" And this was so revealing that we laughed ourselves to tears. From then on it has been very hard for us to accept that 'the enemy is out there.'*

What a great revelation!

- Another subject to delve further into would be: **we can't see a thought, neither emptiness, nor nothingness** – we can only experience them. The fact that this world is constructed of thought may help us better understand this illusion.

Recent experiments have shown that "the brain doesn't know the difference between what it sees and what it remembers." In other words, to the brain there is no difference whatsoever between reality and fantasy. Wow!

- Another observation is that through conditioning, often times we are unhappy and we must (I use "must" as a chosen path) **decide to be happy, decide to be positive.** I prefer **being content** because it has a smaller wave than *happiness* and therefore it attracts less of the opposite intention – it is all a matter of choice.

If you want to avoid something unpleasant, you are already focusing your energy on the unpleasantness and only in this way can it enter into your reality. Do not fight negativity, just change your focus. This is why I recommend that you focus only on all those things that are positive and pleasant.

● **Supposition creates much annoyance in life.** We suppose so many things about others without having the slightest idea about who the other person really is or what he is trying to say. We cannot enter into somebody else's world. When two people meet, they each have their own world; they don't even touch. They create a **third,**

shared reality and there is where they can indeed meet. A positive way to create this third reality starts with respectful communication and creating common realities. This is where we start feeling good because from here mutual empathy and affinity arise.

Our essence has many aspects. Each person we come into contact with connects with one of our unknown aspects. This way, many **shared realities** are created – each one of which is **absolutely unique**. However, the ego does not accept that these new worlds are independent from each other, because it believes its own existence can only be validated by comparing and judging – thus creating jealousy and envy.

• A thought that carries something quite profound: **He who seeks is what he seeks.** It's a paradox. We are God without knowing that we are God, living God. This leads me to ponder how God communicates with us. All of life is energy in the form of waves. Each wave has an upper part and a lower part. We accept that what is above is positive and what is below is negative. So where the negative crosses the positive – be it upward or downward – there are meeting points which form a straight line and here God 'awaits' information, so He is always informed. All of this is very paradoxical as well and very hard to understand. But once this has been accepted as a fact it is much easier to comprehend the incomprehensible, see the invisible, feel the unfelt and hear the unspoken.

Xamanda, regarding this subject, I recall an experience: once in a workshop with an American native shaman we spoke about poetry. Since I do not care much for poetry, I paid attention to what people were saying 'between the lines' and I had a lot of fun.

I think that if you can read between lines in this book, you are also going to have a lot of fun.

- One other thing is **does free will exist?** As we can see, for the ego it sure does not, because it gives many arguments and reasons to justify its existence! We ourselves have written our book in the company of everyone around us, who has given us the possibility of living a very intensive life. We are at the same time, author, director and main actor in our movie.

On the other hand, the ego will surely say *yes* to the following questions:

Does sin exist?

Does karma exist?

Does reincarnation exist? (Needs time!).

Do parallel lives exist? (No need of time!).

Does synchronicity exist?

What really matters is what you believe or what you've been led to believe and how they resonate with your inner self.

• What's interesting is **when the lights go out** in our movie. After so many experiences, the light simply goes out and that is called death. What remains is only the 'blank screen' which has always been there. So death is nothing more than turning off the light. Without light there is no shadow and therefore no life. **We return to Nothingness, the source of Everything**.

But in what state do we leave this earth? I once saw two tombstones; one read: **"born dying"** and the other: **"died while living"** and these are two lives with completely different viewpoints. And I would like each of you to consider what your own tombstone will say.

- An insight I like is: **Everything is in perfect absolute order** – the only "infirmity" is the human being's craze to change something in this order. That is, when we go with the flow, as water flows along the river, we find that life can be quite easy and simple. But if we set our minds on changing something in the flow, unpleasant situations arise.

- Another phrase I like is **comparison needs the past** – the past doesn't even exist, so comparison is another way to complicate life.

- Think a little about **pyramidal structures and hierarchy.** If we take a company which has a name, it really doesn't have any energy in and of itself. Neither do religion, sports clubs, sects, associations, political parties, etc. They need support and nourishment from the energy of their members. Pyramidal or hierarchical structures are fed by the people below. But the ones who offer their energy cannot always receive back what they have contributed to the structure. The highest parts of structure are the narrowest; this is where the great ego games come in: power, competitiveness, plotting, etc. There's great scarcity here. Although these people at the top might make a lot of money they lose most of the essence of happiness. This is something that greatly impacted me, and why I quit participating in pyramidal structures – neither soccer club nor any other association. All of these pyramidal structures suck more energy out of me than I receive. They can't survive because they don't have their **own** energy. But if I do get into one, I do it consciously, giving only as much energy as I want to give, not as requested.

- Another saying that fascinates me is: **whenever someone smashes his finger with a hammer, he never blames the hammer – much less the nail** but when dealing with people, one immediately blames others. Can you see what I mean?

That's right, Xamanda! "To claim your own responsibility!"

One experience that made me feel quite at ease regarding the negative aspect of the Universe, was during a seminar on how to use lie detectors. One night at eleven o'clock, about fourteen of the participants were gathered by the swimming pool and we were talking about certain individual's wickedness in this world. I then said to them: "I think that if we had so much money or power we would also become corrupt." And they answered back: "Oh, no, not at all, no way, we are more ethical, this would never, ever happen!" So we ran an experiment. Each one of us had to think about what would we do with so much money – a million, ten million, a hundred million, billions – and we all obviously were connected to a lie detector while we theorized about it. By the time it was four A.M. we were all crying in shame having discovered that we were not able to handle money and the power it implies – just as anyone else.

What a good example! Since each person is uniquely capable of handling a certain amount of money, each has **his own** limit. This leads us to power and power sooner or later will corrupt us; this is something one should learn in order to come to terms with certain people and understand them – but that doesn't necessarily mean you have to lend them your own energy.

• Another subject has to do with **choosing the role of being a man or a woman.** If we choose being a man, we submit ourselves to certain points of view or conditioning such as: a man has to be strong, he can not cry, he has to protect the woman, he has to provide for the family, etc. Conditioning differs between a man and a woman, therefore they both contribute with a lot of complex aspects.

Now we touched on the subject of sexuality. **Sexuality is just living love or fear on a physical level**. The man has sexuality to be able to procreate etc. while the spiritual side of sexuality enables him to meet his inner self during orgasm. The woman first looks for security and understanding in order to meet her inner self and from there she can open to sexuality. So it is not very simple to get into a relationship. Moreover, adding the 'rights of ownership' (*my* man, *my* woman, "till death do us part" – etc.) creates conflicts with being true to one's self.

If we consider that the man is and always will be the hunter and that the woman is the prey, identifying herself with this natural role; and knowing that she is nearly always the one who actually chooses the man – then there will be more salt and pepper for a very interesting relationship to develop! A healthy relationship is based on cooperation and mutual understanding.

● There's an affirmation I've read someplace that I like a lot, regarding love, which says: **"I love you, not for who you are, but for who I am when I am by your side."** This also applies to friendship, of course. But in partnership it is divine when this sentence can be lived in all its fullness, and naturally, the ultimate would be if each could accept the other as-is.

I only believe in fidelity to myself. Being faithful to oneself leads us to a very happy life and doesn't necessarily exclude fidelity to your partner, but we, ourselves, are the center of it.

- Another way of feeling happy and content in this world is enjoying, feeling and knowing **when more is less.** Therefore if we want more of something, after going past the limit, it will become less. This will translate into being alert; and if we are able to keep the balance and not fall into the trap of wanting more when the result will end up being less, this is the mastery of living.

- Another idea to live this life intensely is being aware that: **if we have 100% of our attention units available to solve one item at a time, the solution is very easy.** If we have many open items, then our capacity of action is very low.

• Another paradoxical situation I've read was a graffiti I found somewhere which read: **what if there was a war and nobody came?** In other words nobody took part in it. Another simple, yet very deep truth. If I don't get caught in somebody else's problems I do not feed energy into it and I healthily take care of my own Universe.

• Another belief in our lives is that **learning is only possible through bad experiences.** I've been learning only through good experiences for many years now, and I strongly confirm that this is absolutely possible.

Xamanda, explain how is it possible for me to understand why there are people who suffer but won't accept any help!

Try to imagine a soul that has been living on 'cloud nine' for millions of years in complete harmony, peace and happiness, who suddenly realizes that disharmony and suffering, in their many expressions, can also be experienced on Earth, based on duality. So, as an alternative to the familiar situation that it experienced for so long, the soul chooses these Earth experiences at any cost. Though upon landing on Earth, the soul cannot remember any of its previous existence unless it connects with its true essence to realize that it wrote its own script. This is another way of experiencing God as a human being: *Why suffer? — Why not?*

The body needs to produce endorphins in order to function. Scientists have now found that this production is possible through positive (green button) **and/or** negative (blue button) emotions. This green/blue button theory makes us reflect. The body could care less what kind of emotion endorphins come from. Therefore, it is our task to understand which button we're pushing to motivate them - green or blue?

Xamanda, some people doubt that they wrote their own book of life. They argue that such a life would be lethargic; everything already predetermined, with nothing left to contribute.

I understand this quite well, because I also had to heal my own doubts. Take into consideration that doubting is one of God's experiences. The fact that you have written the book of your own life removes the possibility of feeding the negative emotions. This Universe has been created out of God's curiosity. When doubt enters my mind, my own inner voice tells me: "Yes, you have written your own book, but you have forgotten what's on the next page." And this allows me to fall back into the flow of life. Besides, you must believe this to be able to agree with it. Well, that's **my** viewpoint.

So now, we will play a game to analyze your personality: If you had to sum up your whole life in just one word, which word would that be?

Enjoy!

Now, if you let yourself fall into that word "enjoy" – feeling it in its full depth, what other word arises?

Being content!

Great! The first word that comes to your mind tells me that your ego is trying to focus on enjoying life by all means – almost obsessively like a vice. The second word comes from your natural essence, which only wants to be content.

So the challenge for you will be to get the delicate balance between these two forces.

What a good and simple analysis, this is exactly the main dilemma of my life! It gets to the point where I even try to enjoy a bad headache! – Instead of resisting a negative experience, I practice asking for more and more pain until finally relief comes. – Living duality!

Hah! Hah! Hah!

3. INTRODUCTION TO ASTROLOGY

Xamanda, in your manuscript you give great importance to the subject of astrology; I too consider it very instructive.

Astrology obeys one of the "laws" of this Universe and it is a science that has been developed over thousands of years by observing the behavior of human beings under the influences of the planets.

When reading a person's natal chart, all of the various influences indicate many details about this person – his character, his behavior, etc. However, this person's pure essence can only be captured like stones in a mosaic. They each have their own value, but the essence – or better yet – the *role* that this person has chosen to live out in this world can only be seen by backing away from the 'mosaic' – the whole is more than the sum of its parts – thus we see the central message.

When reading a natal chart, sometimes it happens that for an instant I believe that *I am* that person. I can grasp a deeper message that sometimes is almost impossible to put into words.

A natal chart divides the sky into a twelve-part circle, each part belonging to one of twelve signs represented by animals, and twelve houses where the planets have their influences. According to their locations, the ten presently known planets have their individual potentials and are usually connected by lines: red (tension), blue (harmony) and sometimes green ("heaven's help").

The circle is divided into four segments. The segment on the left represents the **"I"** – the one on the right represents how you live your **"You"** – the upper one represents the **"head and ideas"** – and the lower one informs us about the person's **"emotions and shadows"** (hidden self). This is the stage where life unfolds.

The ascendant (AC) represents the start of life. Following downward from the AC to the IC (*Imum Coeli*, which represents the person's weaknesses), continuing upward to the DC (Descendant), which together represent the first half of life. During this period, the birth sign (heredity) is the dominant influence. The semicircle from the DC to the MC (Midheaven), then back to the AC, represents the second half of life. During this period the Ascendant (the "*I*") is the dominant influence. The MC informs us about the person's long-term goal.

Along the circle there are four consecutive elements: Fire, Earth, Air, and Water. Three houses belong to Fire (which depends on wood and oxygen), three houses belong to Earth (inert), three houses belong to Air (which is restless), and three houses belong to Water (which eludes capture, needs movement to stay alive).

Within this circle, the planets represent the script and roles of *us*, the actors.

The most important ingredient in astrology is the interpretation of the correspondences of signs, planets, and houses:

- The sign of **ARIES** (fire) has MARS (warrior) as its planet and it rules the first house (how I project myself toward others and how I feel). Within the human body it represents the head. You must imagine that the ram has spent the whole winter at the stable. In spring the shepherd opens the stable and the ram bolts, knocking down three or four fences without even noticing. So one of Aries' characteristics is that he doesn't care if he crashes through a wall. Just like any other sign, Aries also has two aspects: breaking down the wall or choosing to use the door – though sometimes breaking *it* down too!

- The sign of **TAURUS** (earth) has VE-NUS (sensual aesthetics) as its planet and it rules the second house (security, mainly economic). Within the human body it represents the neck. The main characteristic is: *here I am – and I'm not moving until this* *place runs out of grass.* The best stimulus to move him is taunting him with a 'red cape,' or obviously, lack of grass.

- The sign of **GEMINI** (air) has MERCURY (messenger) as its planet and it rules the third house (communication). Within the human body it represents the lungs. Gemini has two faces and his problem is that he hardly ever knows which face is in charge. This is also quite a problem for others. He is a brilliant communicator and always likes to have the last word.

- The sign of **CANCER** (water) has as its planet the MOON (emotions) and it rules the fourth house (home). Within the human body it represents the chest and the stomach. In nature, the crab doesn't have an efficient weapon to defend himself. This is why instead he has his eyes on top, providing a 360-degree view to keep watch over his environment. Another quality is that he is capable of withdrawing very quickly, leaving a void between himself and another (handling a void, for most people, is a difficult thing to do).

- The sign of **LEO** (fire) has the SUN as its planet (I am the king) and it rules the fifth house (pleasures in life, family). Within the human body it represents the heart. Leo depends on others to be king; to be happy he needs a queen. At the time of the harvest, the king takes all the credit and says: *'Look at all **I** have done'*.

- The sign of **VIRGO** (earth) has MERCU-RY (messenger) as its planet and it rules the sixth house (health and profession). Within the human body it represents the intestines. For a Virgo everything must be categorized in boxes and he goes crazy if he finds something in his life that doesn't fit into one of the boxes. He is very methodic and likes to work in an orderly manner.

- The sign of **LIBRA** (air) has VENUS (sensual aesthetics) as its planet and it rules the seventh house (relationships). Within the human body it represents the kidneys. For a Libra it is very important that no one throws him out of balance; he wants to be the center, therefore he reigns.

- The sign of **SCORPIO** (water) has PLUTO (karmic bomb) as its planet and it rules the eighth house (administration of others' estate, sexuality). Within the human body it represents the sexual organs. The scorpion lives under a rock and next to a puddle and it only stings when he is attacked – or feels he's being attacked. He attacks himself when he can't see a way out of a very critical situation in his life.

- The sign of **SAGITTARIUS** (fire) has JUPITER (expansion, abundance) as its planet and it rules the ninth house (philosophy, religion, international travel). Within the human body it represents the thighs. Sagittarius has been sent by God to impose law and order in the world and therefore he is never wrong, i.e., he's always convinced that he is right, because God has sent him!

- The sign of **CAPRICORN** (earth) has SATURN (introversion, humility) as its planet and it rules the tenth house (public stage). Within the human body it represents the knees (surrender). It is said that a Capricorn is born old and dies young. As he stands on top of the mountain, of all the signs he is the one that has the best overview: He doesn't miss a thing and he is erroneously accused of being controlling. He is little understood during his youth, so people challenge him. In view of this, he can either respond by withdrawing defeated, or accept the challenge and win. He doesn't need much to be content.

- The sign of **AQUARIUS** (air) has URANUS (sudden change) as its planet and it rules the eleventh house (friendship). Within the human body it represents the calves. Aquarius has total freedom in the air. Since freedom is the main issue for Aquarius, he constantly looks for freedom instead of living it. He represents freedom without knowing it and this is why he can fall into fears and phobias.

- The sign of **PISCES** (water) has NEP-TUNE (the mystical) as its planet and it rules the twelfth house (difficult trans-formation). Within the human body it represents the feet. Like Aquarius, Pisces has total freedom in the water, but finds it very hard to use. In the sea (freedom) he is afraid and in an aquarium he suffo-cates. His strength is longsuffering. Pisces is always in second place (looking for the role of victim), naturally regretting this situation until, in rare cases, he realizes that second place can be the better place (because it is safer).

The percentage of planets placed in masculine or feminine signs is very im-portant. Fire and air signs are mascu-line; water and earth signs are feminine. Try to imagine a man living in a purely masculine environment, having 70% of his planets in feminine signs! One must realize that *'masculine'* has nothing to do with manhood; it is related to **action** (doing, overcoming obstacles) and *'feminine'* has nothing to do with womanhood; it is related to **inaction** (receptive).

Indeed! After reading your manuscript I was happy to learn the reason for the problems I had being a man having a higher percentage of planets in feminine signs.

While interpreting a natal chart, the following symbols can offer a lot of information about the person's future relationships in a few words:

- Mars represents the father and Venus represents the mother at the time of conception. These influences can be so strong that a woman may look for the characteristics of *her* Mars in a partner and the man will look for a partner with the characteristics of his Venus.

- The Moon supplies information on the emotional status of the mother during labor, and the Sun supplies information regarding the father.

The mother has stronger influence over birth signs in water or earth, whereas the father has the stronger influence over birth signs in air or fire.

With this simple information above, I have been able to read many people's natal charts with good success. Of course intuition helps and sometimes even imagination, but most of all, other peoples' curiosity will make them accessible.

Astrology is capable of giving surprisingly precise information, for example:

Jupiter (expansion, abundance) in conjunction (joined) with Saturn (introversion, humility) in the ninth house and in the sign of Taurus –would possibly signify the following interpretation:

This person does well by frequently taking saunas (expansion) and resting (introversion) at the same time (conjunction). He likes to travel (ninth house) but has to have a home away from home, where he spends most of his time (Taurus). Therefore he doesn't like to jump from hotel to hotel. He tremendously enjoys studying philosophies in depth (ninth house).

The purpose of this whole chapter on astrology is to help you better understand the people around you and/or who cross your path – and above all, to better understand yourself!

EPILOGUE

Xamanda, I have now integrated almost all of the aspects (all the pieces of the mosaic) in your manuscript, and by interpreting it my own way, in some inexplicable way, I felt One with you.

In order to complete my mosaic, I am missing an important point of view and that is

The relationship between the Earth and the human being.

Based on the principle "as it is within so it is without and viceversa", in our introduction to Astrology we gave examples about the correlation there is between planets and the human being; then the earth could also shape man's behavior, couldn't it?

You mention a very interesting point. I'll give you - according to the mosaic concept - different kinds of information on the subject, so that you can present it avoid judging as much as possible. You can draw your own conclusions with the help of your intuition.

- Each country, even each city, has its own horoscope (for instance: Uruguay is Virgo with Pisces rising; USA is Cancer with Sagittarius; Spain is Sagittarius with Aquarius; Switzerland is Virgo with Scorpio, and so on).

- When sensitive people visit different places, they realize they feel differently in each country, even in each city.

- According to our own horoscope, and depending where we are, the astro-chart shows us how our personalities experience transformations. In each one of these cities and countries our strengths and weaknesses express themselves differently.

- Feng-Shui is the art and science of harmony between life and its surroundings, this means that the cardinal points which surround us in our environment will correlate with the human being. It helps us to create an area within which the individual can live in harmony with nature and earth's subtle energy. Feng-Shui shows us in particular, how the surrounding energies resonate within us in order to take them into consideration when we are building homes.

• During a scientific conference I found out that just one volcanic eruption could be more damaging to the environment than what we, the human race, have done to it during the past 60 or 80 years.

• There are places on earth which are famous for being energy points - often connected to one another (the Bermuda Triangle, the Golden Triangle, etc.). Most churches were constructed on these energetic points.

• The calendar system used by the Mayans who were astronomically oriented, consists of different cosmic and terrestrial time cycles. For instance: 18980 days H» 52 years; 144000 days H» 395 years; 5125 years (this is a cycle in which Mayans, Hopis and Vedas all coincide); 25627 years, etc. All of these cycles end on 12.21.2012. Our present fourth age also ends approximately on that date and a fifth one (the one called the age of light) will begin. By then the earth will be aligned with our sun and the center of our galaxy, and also, be directly in the Milky Way's equator.

• There's a permanent electric tension between the ionosphere, which carries a positive charge, and the earth's surface, which has a negative one - that is released through storms. By the same token, there are resonant frequencies (also called Schumann waves) with which the earth starts to oscillate. Until 1983, the lowest resonant frequency was permanently at 7.83 Hertz (which correlates to Theta waves - hypnotic state – therefore, somehow up until now we have been sleeping!).

Lately however, this frequency has been constantly increasing and is now approximately at 12 Hertz (corresponding to Alpha state: relaxed awakened state). It is believed that this Schumann frequency will continue to increase to 13 and 14 Hertz until 2012 (corresponding to Beta waves - the normal awakened state), through which we will experience a transformation in consciousness which will allow us to more easily solve our earthly problems.

Scientific researchers also found that our brain and our heart oscillate at Schumann frequencies as well. The result of these frequency variations is a heightened state of consciousness, which places us (and the earth) in transitory stressful situations. This situation makes us feel that time flies away (until now one day seemed 24 hours long, nowadays it seems equivalent to 14 hours). Since the brain reacts to external energies and vibrations with a new orientation of its internal circuits, we are now open to the possibility of profiting from the unrealized capacities of our subconscious mind. This will be further reinforced by the reversal of the earth's magnetic field.

- Scientists who do brain research have found that certain information exists (for example, lifting an arm) seconds **before** the thought takes place!

• Many natives call the earth "Mother Earth." I feel odd referring to the "mother" subject mentioned earlier in this book. The Bible also mentions the fact that we are made from earth. So, if the earth is our mother, what kind of an influence do we have over her? Furthermore, isn't it exactly the other way around?

Great!! Xamanda, I'm impressed by your sincere response. I'm glad to know that many readers will have the opportunity to be inspired by this book and write their own, and in this way they will learn to better understand and love themselves. By understanding their world and themselves better, important things become less so, thus minimizing actual reality and the blows of the dual counterbalancing forces. And as a result: obtain a satisfying life.

To close, some final words; I'd like to quote a famous painter friend of mine:

"What makes this rose so beautiful? The strength of its beauty is mainly born of the surroundings it's connected to, and not just of itself. Whatever is around it is part of the rose".